A New Model
For
Biblical Studies

Dr. Charles R. Vogan Jr., Ph.D.

ISBN   978-0-6151-3935-7

Ravenbrook Publishers

A subsidiary of

Shenandoah Bible Ministries

www.shenbible.org

A New Model For Biblical Studies

Human knowledge is, by definition, flawed. We hate to admit that, but it's true simply because we can't know all things. Therefore our account even of the most perfect system will not only lack a great deal of information that we can't take in, it may just be skewed and not in line with the reality of the thing.

The same holds true for our understanding of the Bible. Few people, particularly Bible students and scholars, would admit that they may have a flawed understanding of God's Word. Our writings about the Bible tend to take on the authority of the Bible itself. By virtue of having touched the divine, our limited experience of it takes on the divine aura and does not willingly open itself to questioning. Tradition and human authority are often necessary safeguards to preserve the truth; but at times they can be impediments to learning or to correcting our artificial versions of the truth.

All human endeavor is open to question, correction, and realignment. Only God himself and his Word are perfect. In our limitations we make systems or models to help us understand God, this reality that is bigger than we are. But we can tell when our models break down – we can tell they have limitations – when they don't meet our needs. There are times when the Word of God must "teach, rebuke, correct and train" all of us. (2 Timothy 3:16)

The function of a model

The Bible is too large a book to grasp without using some sort of method to organize its many parts. Unless you are the type of person who just reads in it here and there, hit and miss, and you're not concerned with trying to put it all together into a meaningful message, then you're going to use some sort of model to organize it.

A "model" is a device that engineers, artists, and other professionals use to help them get a handle on a big project. For

3

example, architects will build a scale model of a skyscraper before they attempt the real thing – it's cheaper, and they can work out the problems in the model instead of ruining the actual building with unforeseen mistakes. Then they use that model as a guide for construction.

Scholars also build their own "model" to help them understand and work with the Bible. They have some fundamental questions they want answers for: first, what is the Bible itself? What's going on in the stories of the Bible? Is God working on some specific project in his Creation? Is there a goal for that project? How much progress has been made? How does man fit into the picture? Can we get an overall idea of the "big picture" in the Bible? If the Bible is going to answer these questions for us, we need to find some way of organizing and categorizing its data that will yield the right answers.

Another example of using a model or method of interpretation on a system of data is in the field of science. Newton gave the world an amazing set of equations that precisely explained the way gravity and motion and mass interact with one another. Armed with these equations, scientists set out describing our world for the next 200 years – very successfully. We were able to use and profit from this research, thanks to the mechanical model of the universe that Newton gave us.

Around 1900, however, scientists were running into brick walls and dead ends using Newton's model. It didn't exactly work in all situations, and nobody knew why. The reason was that Newton's model was imperfect – it wasn't exactly the right way of looking at things *if you wanted the whole truth*. It served its purpose in limited technological situations, and it's still useful in many ways; but it's not the best way to look at the whole universe if you want to learn exactly how it works. Einstein, Bohr, Planck and others gave us a new model that fits the facts more exactly.

The same is true with the Biblical models that the Church has been using for several hundred years. While they were useful in their time, modern science, Liberalism, non-Biblical religions, and a host of other forces in our world have since then been straining the old models to their breaking point. The Church no longer has relevant answers to today's problems. She no longer has the authority to speak to these issues, and therefore has lost the respect she once had in our society. It used to be that when the Church spoke, people listened. But now even those within the ranks of the Church are in utter confusion about what the truth really is.

So what we have now in the Church are a lot of traditions being passed down from generation to generation, without much new work being done to better understand the original document – the Bible. Most Bible studies are simply the rehashing of old theories. Even teachers, who ought to be studying the Bible intensely for themselves to make themselves masters of the text, usually just pass on to their students what was passed on to them. Without questioning whether their version is correct, the Sunday School lessons from a hundred years ago are still held up as the core lessons of the Bible to new students under a superficial cover of modernity.

This is our strategy for reaching a sophisticated world that no longer takes the Church or its ministry seriously. We have lost *authority* in our ministry, largely because we think we can carry over antiquated traditions without doing new research in Biblical studies. The Liberals, seemingly, are the only ones doing new research now – unfortunately they're discovering reasons to do away with the Bible. While our culture has shed its respect for authority of all kinds, and no longer puts a value on life and morals and the principled life, Christians haven't been ready with a convincing argument to the contrary – from the pages of the Bible. It's distressing to see these battles raging on a national level: the unbelievers are dumping morals and values, and almost the only argument that Christians use to counter the trend is that "we've always had these morals and values." And because that's an insufficient argument, the unbelievers are winning these legal battles.

So it makes a great deal of difference *how* you interpret the Bible. It may be that the methods you use to study it actually turn it into a useless document, leaving more questions unanswered than before.

The time has come for a new model to use in reading the Bible. If it really is a book of answers about God and man, then we ought to be getting the *same* answers from it – no matter who reads it. The only way to account for the myriad of theories that people get from the Bible is that the old models don't work anymore in the face of our modern crises.

Progressive Revelation

One model or way of interpreting the Bible is the idea of Progressive Revelation. It's a theory that has been around for quite some time. Here is a quote from the theologian Charles Hodge, professor at Princeton Seminary in the Nineteenth Century:

> The progressive character of divine revelation is recognized in relation to all the great doctrines of the Bible … All that is in a full-grown tree was potentially in the seed. All that we find unfolded in the fullness of the Gospel lies in a rudimental form in the earliest books of the Bible. What at first is only obscurely intimated is gradually unfolded in subsequent parts of the sacred volume, until the truth is revealed in its fullness.[1]

Let's look at the theory of Progressive Revelation. According to the theory, our Christian faith consists primarily of several key events: the incarnation of Christ, the death of Christ, his resurrection, our faith in him, deliverance from our sin, and uniting with him in Heaven. And we learned of these events, of course, in the New Testament – it's there that the essential facts of Christ shine brilliantly. We use the stories that teach of these events in evangelistic services to bring more people to Christ; we use the Letters of the Apostles in Sunday School lessons and Bible studies to better explain our faith to our students. The New Testament aims right at the root issue – the necessary elements of true salvation in Christ.

On the other hand (according to the theory), the Jews only had shadows to work with. Since Jesus had not yet come, they knew God only in a limited way. They were expected to live up to what they *did* know, but the elements of their faith consisted in the Temple, animal

---

[1] Charles Hodge – **Systematic Theology**, Vol. 1; Wm. B. Eerdmans Publishing Co.; reprinted 1975; p. 446.

sacrifices, the land of Canaan – hardly a comparison to the richness of the Christian faith. That makes the Old Testament, then, a book of limited use to Christians. It didn't save the soul – or even adequately illuminate the mind – of the Israelite, so a Christian has to be careful of relying too much on a Jewish book.

It's not as if the Old Testament were perfectly useless to us, though. There is a thread of eternal truth weaving in and out of the stories that we Christians can detect. The theory is this: at the beginning of the Old Testament, particularly with Genesis 3, we are shown a faint glimpse of things to come. When God pronounced Satan's doom, he predicted the time when the woman's "offspring" would come and "crush your head" – perhaps a reference to Christ. This was the beginning of what Bible scholars have called the "scarlet thread" running throughout the Old Testament and culminating in the New Testament account of Christ.

As the Old Testament progresses, each story adds a little more to the picture of the process of salvation. Or should we say that the picture grows clearer as time goes on. We could illustrate it in this way:

| Abraham | Moses | David | Prophets | Christ |

Figure One – Progressive Revelation

The stories of Abraham, Moses and Mt. Sinai, Joshua and the conquest of Canaan, the Judges, David and his descendants, and the Prophets all help to bring the picture into sharper focus. But obviously we can't stop anywhere along the way and claim that we have a true idea of what we need for our Christian faith.

In other words, we are given little bits and pieces to the secret of salvation through Christ all through the Old Testament. An observant Jew would have been collecting these pieces over the ages, and could have guessed that it was leading up to *something* in the future, though he wouldn't know exactly what. It's always been a question as to how much the Israelites knew about the process of salvation. Could they be saved? Did their limited knowledge and limited access to God do anything for their eternal souls? At the very least, however, the careful Jew should have been willing to listen to Christ when the Lord came, though he would not have understood what he already had well enough to be saved himself.

That's the theory of Progressive Revelation. On the surface it seems to fit the facts. But when one probes a bit deeper, there are some disturbing realities that the theory doesn't fit.

Let's turn to one of the leading early proponents of this theory, Geerhardus Vos – a professor of the new field of Biblical Theology at Princeton Theological Seminary. In his inaugural address at Princeton in 1894, he stated the following.

> The truth of revelation, if it is to retain its divine and absolute character at all, must be perfect from the beginning. Biblical Theology deals with it as a product of a supernatural divine activity, and therefore bound by its own principle to maintain the perfection of revealed truth in all its stages. [2]

This is a good start, but within the self-imposed restraints of Progressive Revelation it never reaches a useable fulfillment until the very end.

> … the advance in revelation resembles the organic process, through which out of the perfect germ the perfect plant and flower and fruit are successively produced. [3]

---

[2] Geerhardus Vos: **Redemptive History and Biblical Interpretation**, "The Idea of Biblical Theology", Presbyterian and Reformed Publishing Co.; 1980; p. 10-11.

[3] Ibid., p.11.

This is an unfortunate analogy. Vos emphasizes the *organic* nature of revelation throughout the Old Testament. Did he miss the point that the only useable stage of a wheat plant or fruit tree is the last one? Until that stage happens, the plant is taking up space and not of any benefit! Perhaps he feels the inadequacy of the Old Testament stories for his Christian faith.

> The Gospel of Paradise is such a germ in which the Gospel of Paul is potentially present; and the Gospel of Abraham, of Moses, of David, of Isaiah and Jeremiah, are all expansions of this original message of salvation, each pointing forward to the next stage of growth, and bringing the Gospel idea one step nearer to its full realization. [4]

The "full realization," of course, would be Christ. But in what way was the Gospel as we know it (Vos *did* say that the seed is a perfect encapsulation of the full fruit) at Paradise? How did the Gospel benefit Abraham, Moses, David, Isaiah and Jeremiah with their limited experience? Is not salvation as we know it in Christ an experience of the NT Church? Is someone truly saved short of experiencing Christ himself? Where did the "full realization" in Christ put the OT saints, as far as their souls were concerned? Either the Old Testament saints benefited in a real way from salvation in Christ through this "Gospel" they had, or they had an unusable form of the Gospel. One can say that the Gospel was "potentially present," but what do such words actually mean?

Is this really the best model to fit the data? Or is it actually confusing the issue, shutting doors (practically, if not theoretically) to investigation into valuable material for our Christian faith?

Vos' "organic" concept of Scripture is totally artificial. He means by it, the gradual growth of a germinal idea from embryo to mature form. He then uses the Covenant as an example: it also takes such an "organic" path – the Covenant idea being the basis of God's

---

[4] Ibid.

dealing with man at Creation, the Covenant with Abraham, the Covenant at Sinai, the Covenant with Israel that "gives rise to prophecy," and finally the new Covenant brought to light through the shedding of Jesus' blood. In other words, the Covenant as *we* use it is only found in Christ. The rest of the saints of the Bible had to use an undeveloped form (though as Vos points out, perfect in itself, as a child resembles a man).

The only way one can call it an "organic growth" is to close one's eyes to the huge, complex structure of the Old Testament and trace an arbitrary line of thought along a narrow path, like shining a light on a path at night while surrounded by a forest. In fact the evolutionists do this very thing: they arbitrarily pick out a "path" of evolution through God's Creation, claiming that one link leads to another; whereas the truth is that each "link" turns out to be what scientists call a "singularity" – an event standing on its own, best understood in its context, and not necessarily a stepping stone to a more developed idea. Progressive Revelation lends itself better to evolutionary theory, a fact that the Liberals have not failed to exploit.

Actually the Covenant is fully developed in the Old Testament. The only new concept that the New Testament adds to the picture is the person "Jesus" who administers the Old Testament Covenant, as it is fully described there, to his people. Paul considered the Old Testament not as an organic development of immature ideas that only find fruition in Christ as we find him in the New Testament, but a textbook of the doctrines of Christ that, in themselves, *fully* instruct God's people on the truth of Christ – to the point that they can be saved by means of them.

> ... the holy Scriptures [*to Paul, the Old Testament*], which are **able to make you wise for salvation through faith in Christ Jesus**. (2 Timothy 3:15)

On the contrary, it's easy to demonstrate that the doctrine of shedding blood for sin is in Genesis 4, along with the substitution of a victim for man's sin. The concept of the resurrection is in Genesis 22 (we are told, in Hebrews 11:19, that Abraham learned the doctrine there). The concept of the sign of the Covenant – the circumcised heart

– is in Deuteronomy 10:16. Almost all of our uniquely Christian doctrines are found in full form in the Old Testament, requiring no further "organic" development. The only reason that many don't see them there is because the name "Jesus" isn't labeled on every story.

The "old" Covenant?

The fatal flaw to the theory of Progressive Revelation is that this makes the Old Testament almost unnecessary to the Christian. Why bother with a blurry picture when we have the "full revelation" in the New Testament? If the New Testament gives us everything we need for faith and salvation in Christ, why settle for less in the bits and pieces of the Old Testament stories? As the theory's proponents are quick to point out –

> In the past God spoke to our forefathers through the prophets *at many times and in various ways*, but in these last days he has spoken to us *by his Son*, whom he appointed heir of all things, and through whom he made the universe. (Hebrews 1:1-2)

And they also point to another passage in Hebrews that seems to strengthen their case. We are told that God disposed of the Old Testament system and replaced it with the New Testament system.

> But the ministry Jesus has received is as superior to theirs as the covenant of which he is mediator is *superior to the old one*, and it is founded on better promises. For if there had been nothing wrong with that first covenant, no place would have been sought for another … By calling this covenant "new," he has made *the first one obsolete*; and what is obsolete and aging will soon disappear. (Hebrews 8:6-7,13)

But now we have two problems. People reject the authority of the Old Testament over them because they think this passage equates the Law (and by association, the Old Testament) with the "first covenant." Let's clear that up first.

The Law was not the "first covenant." This is a superficial way of looking at the Bible. To get the real meaning of the Hebrews passage, we have to keep reading. The next verse solves the problem.

> But God found fault with the *people* and said: "The time is coming, declares the Lord, when I will make a new covenant with the house of Israel and with the house of Judah. It will not be like the covenant I made with their forefathers when I took them by the hand to lead them out of Egypt, because they did not remain faithful to my covenant, and I turned away from them, declares the Lord. This is the covenant I will make with the house of Israel after that time, declares the Lord. *I will put my laws in their minds and write them on their hearts.* I will be their God, and they will be my people." (Hebrews 8:8-10)

If you know something about Old Testament history, you will recognize this reference to the Exodus and Mt. Sinai. God brought his people out of Egypt and made them his nation; he would be their God, and they would obey his Law. At Mt. Sinai he gave them his Law through Moses. There was nothing wrong with the Law – it was a perfect statement of God's holiness and the kind of life that he expected out of his people. Without the Law there would be utter chaos in his Kingdom, as there would be in any kingdom that is lawless. The difficulty of the Law is seen in this passage:

> And if we are careful to obey *all* this Law before the LORD our God, as he has commanded us, *that* will be our righteousness. (Deuteronomy 6:25)

Righteousness is the qualification for living in God's Kingdom. If you're righteous, you can stay; if you're not righteous, then you must be punished or eliminated. At Mt. Sinai, what the Israelites learned is that they must follow this Law to the letter if they wanted to be counted righteous. That was the "old Covenant" – they themselves had to keep the Law. And as they proved so eloquently in their subsequent history, it's impossible! Nobody can follow this Law perfectly. That's why Hebrews 8:8 states that God found fault with the *people*, not his Law.

There's only one man in history that has successfully followed the Law to the letter, and that's Christ himself. The rest of us simply can't live up to that high standard. Yet God will never relax the standard, because he won't tolerate a Kingdom full of unrighteous subjects. Impossible or not, we are still obligated to keep God's Law.

But if someone can *make* us righteous, that would also satisfy God's requirement. This is in fact what Jesus does for us. He takes the burden of obedience to the Law from our backs, fulfills the Law in our place, and then gives us his righteousness as a gift. Now we can freely enter God's Kingdom without fear of rejection.

But he also must make provision for our continuing in righteousness, so he fills us with his Spirit to drive us, mold us, move us to live according to God's Law. We can't do it on our own, but Jesus, as he lives in our hearts, will draw us after him in conformity to the Law of God – so that we will never be rejected.

And that is what it means when Hebrews says, "I will put my laws in their minds and write them on their hearts." The Law has not changed, nor has the requirement to live according to the Kingdom Law changed. What has changed is this: who is going to make this happen in us? The Israelites themselves had to follow the Law, and they failed; we Christians rely on Christ to conform us to God's Law. This is the "new Covenant" – Jesus will do it for us. The end result is the same – perfect righteousness – but the means is different. Only the Christian can achieve, in Christ, a perfect righteousness by the Law's standard.

The Prophets longed for this day:

I will give you a new heart and put a new spirit in you; I will remove from you your heart of stone and give you a heart of flesh. And I will put my Spirit in you and *move you to follow my decrees and be careful to keep my laws*. (Ezekiel 36:26-27)

Paul, who had a profound understanding of both the Law and Christ, never set the two in contradiction. He had a high respect for the

Law. But he also knew that we could never keep the Law on our own. The solution is that Jesus would keep the Law for our sake and change us to satisfy the Law's requirements.

> Therefore, there is now no condemnation for those who are in Christ Jesus, because through Christ Jesus the law of the Spirit of life set me free from the law of sin and death. For what the Law was powerless to do in that it was weakened by the sinful nature, God did by sending his own Son in the likeness of sinful man to be a sin offering. And so he condemned sin in sinful man, *in order that the righteous requirements of the Law might be fully met in us*, who do not live according to the sinful nature but according to the Spirit. (Romans 8:1-4)

So, the Old and New Testaments aren't contrary to each other, nor do they teach different doctrine. The contrast in Hebrews 8 isn't referring to the "Old and New Testaments" as they are called in our Bibles. The contrast is in how the Israelites were to achieve righteousness and how we are to achieve it. They were supposed to follow all the Law's requirements; we trust in Jesus to do it for us. And as we learn in Romans 4, the way of faith actually predates the Law, as we learn in Abraham's story, which means that God always did mean for us to do this through Christ!

Limitations of this model

The theory of Progressive Revelation has other major problems.

• The Gospel as we Christians understand it is not just a New Testament concept. Almost the entire Gospel was first worked out in Old Testament history. Though modern scholars only see a "germ" there in the Old Testament, the Apostles saw the full-fledged Gospel [5] – the "good news"

---

[5] See Galatians 1:6-9 for Paul's definition of the Gospel, and the anathema he calls upon those who preach anything different while calling it the "Gospel." One would assume, therefore, that he would not have accepted a definition of the Gospel that makes the Old Testament version of it anything less than what Christians understand it to be.

about Christ and salvation through him – even in the earliest stories. Jesus and his Apostles taught that the Old Testament saints understood the point about Christ and salvation through him.

> The Scripture foresaw that God would justify the Gentiles by faith, and announced the *Gospel* in advance to Abraham: "All nations will be blessed through you." (Galatians 3:8)

Note in this passage that Paul not only claims that Abraham knew about the Gentiles coming into the Kingdom of God, but also the means of their communion – *justification* (which can only be done by the sacrifice of Christ) *by faith* (before the Law). The Gospel consists of nothing less than this, if the word means anything at all. Therefore, the essentials of the Christian Gospel were declared to Abraham at the very beginning – in Genesis 12. It wasn't just a hint of things to come; the core idea of the doctrine was imparted to the Patriarch. That core idea hasn't changed in the least from his time to ours.

The other essentials of our Christian faith are distributed throughout the Old Testament, from beginning to end. Saving faith, the sacrifice that takes away sin, the requirements of the Law that define true righteousness, the King and his Kingdom, deliverance, the Promised Land, the nation of God's special people, communion with God, justification, sanctification, the work of the Spirit – one wonders what scholars really want when they say that only in the New Testament is our faith made clear! And it doesn't appear that there is any "organic" growth to these concepts; the full-blown doctrines of our faith are found even in the most "primitive" times of Israel's history. If anything, the later Prophets called for Israel to return to those simpler times and doctrines!

•   When we minimize the OT stories, we are throwing away the very material that we need to make definitive statements on key issues.

For example, the Creation account in Genesis (along with the expansions and interpretations of Creation found in the rest of the Old Testament) is the best possible explanation of how God created the world. Nothing that modern science offers us can come even close to adequately describing how Creation happened and what was involved in the making of the world. The concept of "command," for instance, found in Genesis 1 ("Let there be …") is the foundation stone for the reign of God over his world, our service to him, morality, and the necessity of judgment. The instruments of science will never detect that spiritual force behind the material universe; yet it is there nevertheless, guiding the destiny of God's universe.

But if the OT is simply a collection of "myths" and traditions (at worst), or an immature or scientifically naïve mind trying to grasp what is mostly beyond his reach, then we would be forced to treat the Creation account as immature or a myth and turn to science to give us a better account. As a matter of fact, the OT gives us vital information for many key issues like this one; we need a vigorous understanding of the book that will recognize its first-level relevance to these issues. Watering it down in any way takes away the Church's ammunition in its war against unbelief.

•   Progressive Revelation also conveniently ignores the fact that the Jews *were* accountable for their rejection of Christ. It wouldn't be fair to condemn the Jews for rejecting Christ if all they had was an imperfect knowledge of the salvation of God. How could they be held accountable if they had no idea that the bits and pieces they had in their Scriptures were actually pointing to the man Jesus? Yet, that's precisely what Christ, Paul and the Apostles did –

they condemned the Jews for rejecting what they should have known.

You diligently study the Scriptures because you think that by them you possess eternal life. *These are the Scriptures that testify about me*, yet you refuse to come to me to have life. (John 5:39-40)

Abraham replied, '*They have Moses and the Prophets; let them listen to them.*' 'No, father Abraham,' he said, 'but if someone from the dead goes to them, they will repent.' He said to him, 'If they do not listen to Moses and the Prophets, they will not be convinced even if someone rises from the dead.' (Luke 16:29-31)

You are in error because *you do not know the Scriptures* or the power of God. (Matthew 22:29)

"You are Israel's teacher," said Jesus, "and *do you not understand these things?*" (John 3:10)

What Israel sought so earnestly it did not obtain, but the elect did. The others were hardened, as it is written: "*God gave them a spirit of stupor*, eyes so that they could not see and ears so that they could not hear, to this very day." (Romans 11:7-8)

For you, brothers, became imitators of God's churches in Judea, which are in Christ Jesus: You suffered from your own countrymen the same things those churches suffered from the Jews, who killed the Lord Jesus and the prophets and also drove us out. *They displease God* and are hostile to all men in their effort to keep us from speaking to the Gentiles so that they may be saved. In this way they always heap up their sins to the limit.

The wrath of God has come upon them at last. (1 Thessalonians 2:14-16)

I will make those who are of the synagogue of Satan, *who claim to be Jews though they are not, but are liars* – I will make them come and fall down at your feet and acknowledge that I have loved you. (Revelation 3:9)

This isn't exactly the language of reconciliation! The Jews were supposed to have gotten the point of Christ – so much so that they were condemned for not believing in him.

I have great sorrow and unceasing anguish in my heart. For I could wish that I myself were cursed and cut off from Christ for the sake of my brothers, those of my own race, the people of Israel. Theirs is the adoption as sons; theirs the divine glory, the covenants, the receiving of the Law, the temple worship and the promises. Theirs are the patriarchs, and from them is traced the human ancestry of Christ, who is God over all, forever praised! Amen. *It is not as though God's Word had failed. For not all who are descended from Israel are Israel.* (Romans 9:2-6)

Therefore, they must have had an adequate description of him in their Scriptures – the Old Testament. It does not fail to describe Christ to us in clear terms for salvation through him. The problem wasn't that they had an unusable picture (an "embryo" without fruit), but they failed to respond with faith to the adequate picture they did have. The doctrine was all there. On that basis they stand condemned.

Notice that there were some Jews who did get the picture. Hebrews 11 lists a number of Old Testament saints who by faith saw Christ, even in their own day.

All these people were still living by faith when they died. They did not receive the things promised; they only saw them and welcomed them from a distance. And they admitted that they were aliens and strangers on earth. People who say such things show that they are looking for a country of their own. If they had been thinking of the country they had left, they would have had opportunity to return. Instead, they were longing for a better country – a Heavenly one. Therefore God is not ashamed to be called their God, for he has prepared a city for them. (Hebrews 11:13-16)

If these saints understood the message of Christ long before he came – in other words, through the revelation of the part of God's Word that they had at the time – then the Jews in Jesus' day were certainly without excuse and entirely at fault for not recognizing him. The Old Testament is sufficient to teach us about Christ.

• In setting aside the Old Testament, that inevitably makes us "New Testament Christians." We believe only in what the New Testament teaches; we teach only the New Testament; and we naturally distrust any serious foray into the Old Testament as leading us away from Christ. This may sound radical, but there are churches that are pointed this way. And many more follow this idea on a practical level, since they rarely teach from the Old Testament (because they don't understand it) but focus their attention almost exclusively on the New Testament. As we shall see below, this cripples our understanding of both Testaments and denies us the riches of God's wisdom and grace for Christian life.

Because they consider the Old Testament to be blurry and fragmentary in nature, even evangelical scholars have had trouble trying to decide what the Old Testament is really teaching. Pastors, therefore, get mixed and confused signals about the OT in their training. The entire OT becomes virtually unusable to the leaders, which message of course gets passed down to the church level. From the top down, Church leaders take a condescending attitude toward the Old Testament – like a concubine in the family. Nobody knows what to do with it: they aren't going to turn it away, but neither are they ready to give it the full authority of Scripture for Christians.

As a matter of fact, most Christians don't go to the OT for anything significant; but instead they regard it as if it were only a history of how we got our present religion – somewhat interesting, but mostly unusable. And you know how much most students love history!

One of the most startling proofs of our practical disdain of the Old Testament is the typical statement of faith. In one leading (conservative) seminary's statement, it begins with the usual nod to all sixty-six books being the inspired Word of God. Next it moves to the fall of the human race into sin through Adam and Eve. Then there is a 2000 year gap – entirely eliminating the Old Testament – as it jumps immediately to the birth of Christ and the Apostolic teachings, which is the focus of the rest of the statement. It's as if the Old Testament doesn't even merit a mention in their testimonial of what they hold to be the truth about God. It's especially telling that a *seminary* would eliminate the whole Old Testament in its statement of faith, in light of the fact that they are supposedly training future pastors and teachers in the Word of God.

It's time we accepted the plain testimony of Christ and the Apostles about the nature and message of the Old Testament.

• There is a lot of confusion about what exactly is the difference between Israelite and Christian. How close did God get to the Israelite? We know that we have God's Spirit in us because of Christ; did the Israelite therefore, who didn't have Christ and had little knowledge of true salvation, enjoy the same grace that we have? How did the spiritual giants of Israel like Moses and David relate to God, without the Christian realities that we now have? And if they didn't have what we take for granted as a basic Christian relationship with God, then can we say that they were "saved" and their names written in Heaven? All these questions and more arise when we draw a hard line between Old and New Testaments and insist that our relationship with God in Christ is strictly a New Testament theme.

• One unfortunate casualty of the practice of setting Old and New Testaments against each other is the subject of faith. Without the depth of the Old Testament lessons, we have reduced faith to simply "believing in Jesus" – a New Testament formula. This too often amounts to saying, "I believe that Jesus can help me with my problems," or "I believe that Jesus loves me when nobody else does," or "I trust Jesus to take care of me in my need." Put on that level, everyone in their right mind will turn to Jesus! That's why modern revivals are able to cater to thousands of hurting people looking for someone who cares about them.

Such a simple act as "turning to someone who cares," however, makes faith a work of man. Anybody can do it. But what if Jesus doesn't come through? What if the problems of life continue, and no prayers are answered? This fact accounts for those same thousands who expressed "faith in Christ" turning away from him and the church, not having received what they were looking for. They were looking for the "bread of this world" (John 6:26-27) instead of the spiritual Christ and his unique spiritual treasures. "Try Jesus!" is not the essence of true faith.

On the other hand, the distinct lessons of the Old Testament give a depth and turn to the subject of Christ that make the typical "revivalist" understanding of salvation seem shallow. Faith is no longer an act of man that "makes" God do what we want from him. It becomes a vision, an understanding, of spiritual realities that weighs down from God's world and changes the human condition. It's becoming aware of the glory of God that bows us down in humility and fear and worship. Faith is seeing God's works and responding appropriately to them. It becomes much more an act of God, an encounter with a reality that we didn't see before but is determined to change us because of what it is. Faith therefore is what Paul describes it to be:

> For it is by grace you have been saved, through faith – and this not from yourselves, it is the *gift of God* – not by works, so that no one can boast. For we are God's workmanship, created in Christ Jesus to do good works, which God prepared in advance for us to do. (Ephesians 2:8-10)

Much of what we need to see about God to make faith happen is only found in the Old Testament. A New Testament-only "faith" is really little or no faith at all.

• Another problem area concerns prophecy. Since much of what we consider prophecy is found in the Old Testament, this makes the subject a particularly Jewish one and leaves Christians on the sidelines as little more than interested bystanders. We see in the Prophets an ongoing confrontation between God and his special people, the Israelites. The issues that the Prophets raise concern matters that seemingly have no direct bearing on our Christian faith – their homeland, the Temple, Jerusalem, the Messiah ruling in their midst, the predictions of all nations coming to Jerusalem to worship the Lord there. What are we Christians to do with all this material besides wave the Israeli flag and cheer them on as they rebuild the modern state of Israel, apparently in fulfillment of the ancient prophecies?

But such a narrow view of the scope of the Prophets, again, doesn't square with what the Bible tells us about them. The Prophets were for everyone – Gentiles as well as Jews. Their message is directly relevant to the Church of God:

> And we have the Word of the prophets made more certain, and *you* will do well to pay attention to it, as to a light shining in a dark place, until the day dawns and the morning star rises in your hearts. (2 Peter 1:19)

Interpreting the Prophets in this light can be challenging; it's much easier to relegate their message to the historical context in which they worked. But a little research will show that all the New Testament writers relied heavily on the message of the Prophets for preaching the Gospel of Christ to the nations. If we aren't up to the task, that doesn't therefore mean that we don't need to pay any attention to the Prophets!

• If you assign the Old Testament to a lower level of importance than the New Testament, you are in effect attempting to take away the authority of the Old Testament. It's clear that throughout the entire book we have nothing less than God's Word: "Thus says the LORD." Man therefore has no authority to set it aside, or consider it as anything less than the oracles of God binding on the human mind and conscience. People who do so are usurping God's authority over his own work. And they may be setting it aside for the wrong reasons – perhaps they don't like its message!

Besides, there is no Scripture giving us permission to do away with the Old Testament. There has been no command or teaching from God that would lead us to treat it with any less respect than what was required from the original Israelites who first received it. On the other hand, there are all sorts of New Testament passages that enjoin us to respect and believe the Old Testament in the same way that the Old Testament saints did.

• There are many teachings in the New Testament that are almost impossible to understand without a thorough knowledge of the Old Testament. Many of them are obvious to the Bible student: the ceremony of the Lord's Supper derives from the Passover event recorded in Exodus; the atonement of Christ on the cross is illustrated by the atonement sacrifice in the Temple. But many New Testament stories remain difficult to handle. For example, the story of the Canaanite woman in Matthew 15 is bewildering to the Christian – why in the world did Jesus treat this woman so harshly? Doesn't he have grace on Gentile believers, ourselves included?

We're going to remain puzzled over these stories until we dig through the Old Testament and do some work in the basics of the faith. There are important concepts there – in the case of the Canaanite woman, legal principles binding on God himself – that will perfectly illuminate the problematic New Testament situations. And as this particular story illustrates, these Old Testament principles make possible *our* Christian religion. God deals with us in the same way.

All this is to say that the Progressive Revelation model has turned the Old Testament into an almost useless book to Christians – yet we have no good reason to feel this way about it, and there is abundant evidence that our dismissal of it doesn't square with the facts.

A new model: Distributed Revelation

While it's true that we aren't given the *entire* picture of the process of Salvation in the Old Testament, it's not true that the picture is "blurry" anywhere along the way. The theory of Progressive Revelation seems to fit the bill only because we're drawing the line between the two Testaments in the wrong place. It's not as if the Old and New Testaments are saying different things, nor is it the case that the New replaces the Old or even focuses the Old into something useable for us. The New Testament does indeed give us new information that completes the picture that the Old was painting. What many Christians have failed to recognize is how utterly dependent the New Testament is on the Old Testament.

> ... The holy Scriptures, which are able to make you wise for salvation through faith in Christ Jesus. (2 Timothy 3:15)

Note that Paul claims we can learn about salvation, even have faith in Christ to be saved, from the holy Scriptures – that is, the Old Testament. The Old Testament is exactly suited to describe Christ to us, in a way that is entirely sufficient for our salvation through him. It lacks only two more points to be complete, which we will look at in a minute. But the fact remains that what it does tell us is not blurry, insufficient, misleading, or wrong – it is entirely accurate and useable for the Christian.

The simple fact that the Apostles quoted from it continually during their ministries should show that they relied on it for their preaching of Christ. [6] The modern practice of hardly mentioning the Old Testament at all, and focusing only on selected New Testament quotes as if they were divorced from the themes of the Old Testament, is not in line with Apostolic practice. For that matter, it would justifiably fall under the condemnation of "preaching another Gospel"!

The New Testament assumes that the foundations of our Christian faith were laid down in the Old Testament first. In fact, a careful study of the New Testament writings will reveal that the writers spent little time going over Old Testament themes themselves – as if they relied on their readers to do their homework first in the Old before coming to this new material of the New Testament. It's like taking a college course in calculus: the teacher isn't going to thoroughly review all the math that you are expected to be proficient in already. There's too much to deal with in this new study; students deficient in the basics need to back away and address their deficiencies:

---

[6] One source lists over 350 direct quotes and allusions to Old Testament passages in the Apostolic letters.

We have much to say about this, but it is hard to explain because you are slow to learn. In fact, though by this time you ought to be teachers, you need someone to teach you the elementary truths of God's Word all over again. You need milk, not solid food! (Hebrews 5:11-12)

So if the Old Testament is the first course to take, what exactly is its subject material? *The theme of the Old Testament is Christ himself.* Both Jesus and Paul explained this to us, as we've already seen.

You diligently study the Scriptures because you think that by them you possess eternal life. These are the Scriptures that *testify about me*, yet you refuse to come to me to have life. (John 5:39-40)

… The holy Scriptures, which are able to make you wise for salvation through faith in *Christ Jesus*. (2 Timothy 3:15)

The Old Testament describes Christ, and our relationship to God the Father through him.

The person and work of Christ is a huge, complex spiritual reality. It requires a lot of room to lay out and explore to its depths. Any quick, superficial account of Christ won't do him justice – and neither will it lead us to a saving faith in him. So the Old Testament spreads out the explanation of Christ over two thousand years, throughout the lives of millions of people, across 39 books – one story at a time. Though we're not told this at the beginning of each of the stories, we could preface them all by saying "Now this is another aspect of Christ." The clue that we're not only allowed to do this but required to is the plain teaching of the New Testament about the purpose of the Old.

It's important to remember that God had planned the sacrifice of Christ, and our salvation through him, from the beginning of the world. Before any of the Bible was written, God had the system all worked out.

> You loved me before the creation of the world. (John 17:24)

> For he chose us in him before the creation of the world to be holy and blameless in his sight. (Ephesians 1:4)

> He was chosen before the creation of the world, but was revealed in these last times for your sake. (1 Peter 1:20)

Therefore, when he started on his relationship with Abraham and his descendants, he began building a system that would result ultimately in his eternal goal. Every piece was laid down with wisdom and care.

> I make known the end from the beginning, from ancient times, what is still to come. I say: My purpose will stand, and I will do all that I please. (Isaiah 46:10)

For the instruction of not only the Israelites but also of the Church at large, God laid out the whole story of who Christ is, and the works he does, throughout the Old Testament. It required that much room to do it justice! It took thousands of years, millions of lives, and the complex interplay of men and nations to fully describe the story.

Progressive Revelation claims that God laid down the pieces one at a time in the Old Testament and the system wasn't complete until the NT. In that it is correct. But **Distributed Revelation** (the new model posited here) claims that each piece laid down in the Old Testament was accurate and complete in itself. It is a necessary portion of Christian doctrine that we need for our faith. The New Testament doesn't alter it, focus it, or baptize it into something more useable for Christians – it *depends* on it as it stands.

The genius of this method of describing the person and work of Christ will be apparent with a little thought. The root problem of understanding anything about God is that he is Spirit; he can't be seen, heard, felt or even followed by the ordinary mortal. Many of the aspects of his spiritual world are incomprehensible to the sinful, ignorant mind. So to make it easy to grasp the essentials of what we need to know about God, he cast them in historical events, through the lives of men and women, in pictures and stories, dealing with concrete realities of the world. Like a storybook with pictures for children, the Old Testament puts the reality of God on a level that we can easily see and understand.

And to avoid confusion, he dealt with each essential aspect of salvation in Christ in separate stories. This means that you must go to different passages to get a new facet of the picture of Christ. The separate truths of Christ are strewn and scattered all over the Old Testament, and must be collected and pieced together to form the whole picture.

Eternal truths

Faith, contrary to what too many people believe, is not the strength of one's convictions. It isn't a work of man at all. Since the natural man is in the dark about the true nature of God and his spiritual world, God must turn the light on, so to speak, so that we can see him. **Faith is living in the light of God's world.** God gives us the ability to see spiritual realities.

> But whoever lives by the truth comes into the light, so that it may be seen plainly that what he has done has been done through God. (John 3:21)

> A man who walks by day will not stumble, for he sees by this world's light. It is when he walks by night that he stumbles, for he has no light. (John 11:9-10)

You are going to have the light just a little while longer. Walk while you have the light, before darkness overtakes you. The man who walks in the dark does not know where he is going. Put your trust in the light while you have it, so that you may become sons of light. (John 12:35-36)

God is light; in him there is no darkness at all. If we claim to have fellowship with him yet walk in the darkness, we lie and do not live by the truth. But if we walk in the light, as he is in the light, we have fellowship with one another, and the blood of Jesus, his Son, purifies us from all sin. (1 John 1:5-7)

Faith is as old as the Bible itself. Abraham was commended for his faith, as was Abel in Genesis 4. Faith, we are told in Romans 4, is the family characteristic that draws us all into a true relationship with God through Christ. It came before the Law; it was ordained from the beginning to be the avenue into God's presence. It's a spiritual skill that transcends time and culture, and brings its holder into the presence of the same God – into the spiritual halls of Heaven – no matter what age they live in.

Through the vehicle of faith we are enabled to see spiritual realities as they really are – not clouded or limited by the historical context that we find ourselves in. Paul makes the startling claim that the Old Testament Jews were supposed to have a faith that makes them partakers in the same vision of the truth as we Christians have:

A man is not a Jew if he is only one outwardly, nor is circumcision merely outward and physical. No, a man is a Jew if he is one inwardly; and circumcision is circumcision of the heart, by the Spirit, not by the written code. Such a man's praise is not from men, but from God. (Romans 2:28-29)

The typical Jew was caught up in the physical aspects of his religion – the aspects of the Israelite "cult" as scholars would call it. God deliberately worked out the principles of his Kingdom through the fabric of history and the lives of millions of his people. But occasionally one of the descendants of Abraham was lifted up above the fabric of history – through his faith – to see eternal truths that aren't bound, and certainly are not clouded, by the mists of time and circumstance. Through faith he saw God as he really is.

> It is because *I saw God face to face*, and yet my life was spared. (Genesis 32:30)

> Moses and Aaron, Nadab and Abihu, and the seventy elders of Israel went up and *saw the God of Israel*. Under his feet was something like a pavement made of sapphire, clear as the sky itself. But God did not raise his hand against these leaders of the Israelites; *they saw God*, and they ate and drank. (Exodus 24:9-11)

> With him I speak face to face, clearly and not in riddles; *he sees the form of the LORD*. (Numbers 12:8)

> In the year that King Uzziah died, *I saw the Lord* seated on a throne, high and exalted, and the train of his robe filled the temple. (Isaiah 6:1)

There are two forms of revelation: natural and spiritual. Natural revelation is what we can learn of the Creator by studying his Creation. Special revelation, however, deals not with Creation and its Maker, but the broken relationship between sinful man and a holy God. We are given new truth from outside the world – from the spiritual world of God. God used history and the lives of people to teach us about these eternal truths; but the medium was not the message itself. This truth is for all nations in all times. And as is the case with the rest of us, only a few Israelites were lifted up above their historical context to see these eternal truths that their own history pointed to. The Spirit showed them the same spiritual realities that we Gentile Christians see.

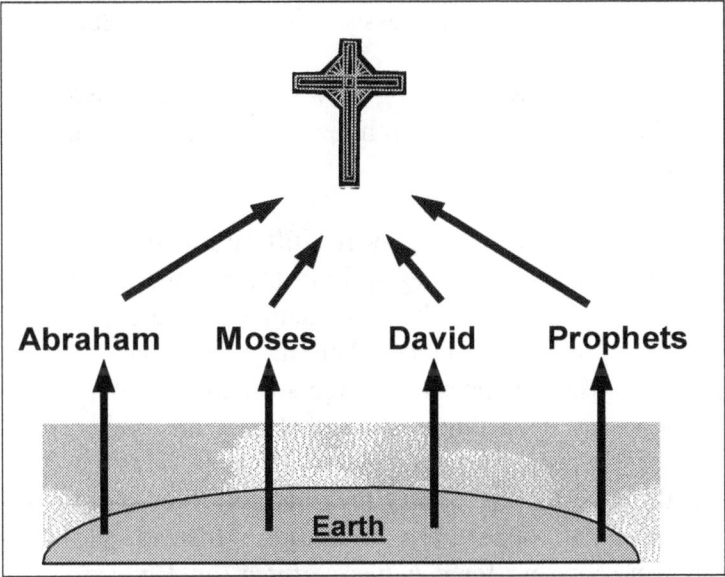

Figure Two – Faith sees the eternal Christ

God has revealed it to us by his Spirit. The
Spirit searches all things, even the deep things of
God. For who among men knows the thoughts
of a man except the man's spirit within him? In
the same way no one knows the thoughts of God
except the Spirit of God. We have not received
the spirit of the world but the Spirit who is from
God, that we may understand what God has
freely given us. This is what we speak, not in
words taught us by human wisdom but in words
taught by the Spirit, expressing spiritual truths in
spiritual words. (1 Corinthians 2:10-13)

Faith is faith, no matter how much information we might have
at the time. Whether we consider Abel who was shown what
constitutes a true sacrifice, or David who followed a specific program
to restore God's Kingdom, or Paul who saw the "mystery" of the
Gospel, they all saw the reality of God in some form. What they saw
isn't in any way different from what we see, when we see God through

our faith. Any saint, no matter when in the historical spectrum, sees the *truth* as it is in Jesus. Anything less wouldn't be saving faith.

> For he was looking forward to **the city with foundations**, whose architect and builder is God. (Hebrews 11:10)

> All these people were still living by faith when they died. They did not receive the things promised; they only saw them and welcomed them from a distance. And they admitted that they were aliens and strangers on earth. People who say such things show that they are looking for a country of their own. If they had been thinking of the country they had left, they would have had opportunity to return. Instead, they were longing for **a better country – a Heavenly one**. Therefore God is not ashamed to be called their God, for he has prepared a city for them. (Hebrews 11:13-16)

> He regarded disgrace for **the sake of Christ** as of greater value than the treasures of Egypt, because he was looking ahead to his reward. (Hebrews 11:25)

> He persevered because he saw **him who is invisible**. (Hebrews 11:27)

Our own faith is not usually attended by an entire grasp of Scripture; how much you know doesn't make it saving faith. Very few people who become Christians know much about the Bible, let alone have a mastery of correct doctrine – that knowledge usually follows later (for some, at any rate!). But someone who is truly converted has seen Christ and his glory, just as the Old Testament saints saw him. It's the vision of the eternal Christ (with or without all the data) that makes the experience of him real. In fact, no doubt many Old Testament saints saw much more in their vision of Christ than we Christians do! Almost everything that we now believe is simply lessons drawn from the Bible, not a direct experience of Jesus himself. This intellectual exercise is something that anybody can do, and is not the mark of true faith.

Hebrews tells us that the Old Testament saints "did not receive the things promised; they only saw them and welcomed them from a distance." (Hebrews 11:13) This doesn't mean that they couldn't see the picture clearly, nor was the picture unusable compared to our view of it. It means that, although they had the data that we also have, they didn't have the motive power yet to make it work. With us, the Son of God brings the reality of God's Kingdom into our hearts, and the Holy Spirit lifts us up to live with Christ.

It's often argued that it's not fair to make Jewish writings read like a Christian manual of doctrine. It's claimed that the Jews saw things from their unique point of view – a point of view that we Christians don't share, and should respect. And to properly understand that viewpoint we have to put our Christian perspective on hold for the time being. But that doesn't agree with the testimony that we have from the New Testament writers, who themselves had the authority to speak to this issue. No less an authority than Christ himself faulted the Jews of his day for not seeing what many would have taken to be a specifically New Testament concept – for example, the doctrine of the "new birth."

"You are Israel's teacher," said Jesus, "and
do you not understand these things?" (John 3:10)

The New Testament writers claim that the Jews had, in their Scriptures, the doctrine of the Gospel as we know it, the Covenant, the true meaning of circumcision, all the information available about the sacrificial system, the Temple and its worship of God – almost everything about Christ that we need to know for salvation. And it tells us how they knew these things: through faith they "saw him who is invisible." The historical context never limited or distorted the eternal truth for the OT saint who had faith.

The Old Testament is not a Jewish perspective on the truth about God. That idea confuses the historical medium with the eternal message. The Old Testament is God's eternal message of salvation written into Jewish history. The purpose of the medium was not to divert them from the eternal message but to instruct them in it. If the Jews were at fault for not recognizing this, then so are modern scholars at fault for perpetuating confusion between the two.

The many aspects of Christ

The Distributed Revelation model tells us that the data about Christ is distributed across all the stories of the Old Testament. We can illustrate it in this way.

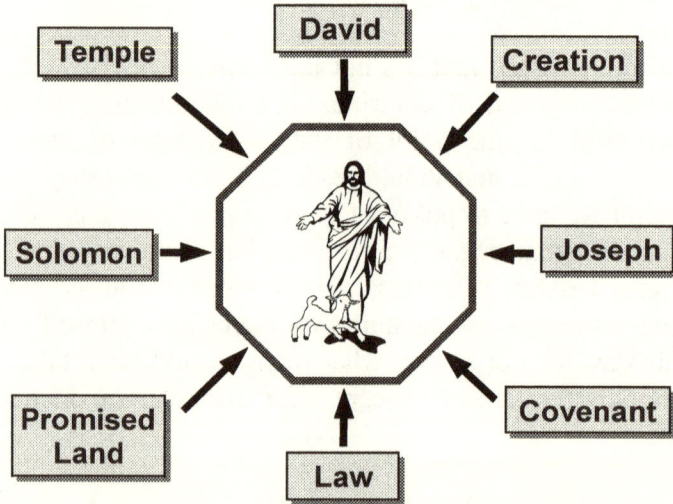

Figure Three – The many aspects of Christ

In any particular story we have the main points of a vital subject laid out for us, clearly and adequately. Let's take the example of *Sacrifice*. In Genesis 4, with the story of Abel and Cain, we learn what the four essentials of an acceptable sacrifice are – the kind of sacrifice that God is pleased with. Here are the four elements:

- A substitute victim
- The firstborn
- Death of the victim – shedding of blood
- Atonement – acceptance from God

The significance of this story is that Abel knew what God required in a sacrifice. His brother Cain brought the wrong kind of sacrifice; through faith, however, Abel brought the kind of sacrifice that met God's requirements for the forgiveness of sin. This was long before the Mosaic Code specified the kind of sacrifice that would take away the Israelites' sins!

> In fact, the Law requires that nearly everything be cleansed with blood, and without the shedding of blood there is no forgiveness. (Hebrews 9:22)

There is only one way that Abel would have known about the expectations of God – and Hebrews tells us.

> By faith Abel offered God a better sacrifice than Cain did. By *faith* he was commended as a righteous man, when God spoke well of his offerings. And by faith *he still speaks*, even though he is dead. (Hebrews 11:4)

It's very questionable whether Adam and Eve knew about true sacrifice from God's perspective; if they had, both sons would have therefore known and Cain wouldn't have offered an unacceptable sacrifice. So Abel was given "inside information" through his faith to enable him to approach God in the right way. What this shows is that even the simplest faith, even the faith of any of the Old Testament saints, will see the same truth in God that we see. Faith dwells in eternal dwellings, not in the shadow land of the historical process.

Notice that the rest of the Bible uses these *same four points* whenever it discusses an acceptable sacrifice to God. There are many other kinds of sacrifices and offerings, for different purposes, mentioned in Scripture; but the fundamental sacrifice that atones for our sins and reconciles us to God is patterned after this story of Abel. The sacrificial system in the Mosaic Law is firmly based on these four principles. The sacrifice of Christ is nothing other than this pattern from Genesis 4 which Abel first learned.

Nothing in the basic structure of an acceptable sacrifice has changed over thousands of years of Biblical history and theology! So Abel still teaches us ("he still speaks") what the essentials of an atoning sacrifice are.

In the same way, we find clear doctrinal lessons on each aspect of the work of Christ all through the Old Testament. Jesus preserves his people from destruction, as described carefully in the story of Joseph. The four important aspects of redemption through Christ are found in the story of Ruth. King Jesus, the Son of David, has five points on his agenda as he builds his Kingdom – the same five points that we first learn about in the story of King David and what he was called to do for Israel. [7]

In a startling example of this principle, we find the four elements of the Gospel of Christ first preached to Abraham through the Covenant that God made with him. And Abraham knew about Jesus – the ultimate Son through whom this Covenant would be extended to God's children around the world!

> Your father Abraham rejoiced at the thought of
> seeing my day; he saw it and was glad. (John 8:56)

One of the most fruitful sources of the revelation of the person and work of Christ in the Old Testament is the list of his many names. Each name describes something about him. For example, the "LORD our Righteousness" teaches us that, instead of trying to become righteous on our own, the Lord Jesus himself will get righteousness for us and cover our sins with it. One list enumerates almost 150 names of Christ throughout the Bible – a rich source of information about Jesus

---

[7] Some may feel that we are describing a resurrection of the old hermeneutical practice of the Church Father Origen – that we see allegories in every Old Testament story. Allegories are spiritualized *applications* of the passage, oftentimes fanciful (as were Origen's). Allegories aren't bad in themselves; but it's safer to let the Apostle tell us where they are in Scripture (see Galatians 4:22-31 for an example). Abel's sacrifice, however, outlines the same *doctrinal* elements that we have in the Mosaic Law and the sacrifice of Christ. These doctrinal analyses, broken down into separate and identifiable headings, are the unique contribution of the Old Testament to the study of Christ.

and his work. Again, the Old Testament is the *only source* of information on many of these names. Far from being a blurry picture of Christ, or unusable for our Christian faith, we have been enjoined to call upon those names when we need those particular treasures in our lives. (Joel 2:32)

It's important to notice that each story, each facet, each passage dealing with a distinct part of the picture is perfectly clear in itself. There is nothing blurry in the picture. Nowhere in the New Testament will you find such a simple, one-two-three layout of the facts as you do in the Old Testament story. Nothing in the rest of the Bible will contradict the message of the passage you are studying; in fact, the Bible will rely on the fact that you mastered the message of that story and it now forms a vital part of your Christian world view.

This is different from Progressive Revelation, which claims that the picture was always blurry and unclear in the Old Testament, unreliable in itself to save the soul, and that only the New Testament shows us the clear picture of Christ. **Distributed Revelation** requires us to search the entire Bible for the facts of Christ. A so-called "New Testament Christian" is missing most of the picture!

A child's toy can be used to illustrate the difference between the two models. In the following diagram, there are two disks held together in the center with a tack. There are windows cut out in the top disk, and the windows are turned so as to expose parts of the pictures underneath on the second disk. The trouble is that there's not enough information in each window to show you what's really going on – it's easy to draw the wrong conclusions about the pictures with the windows in this position.

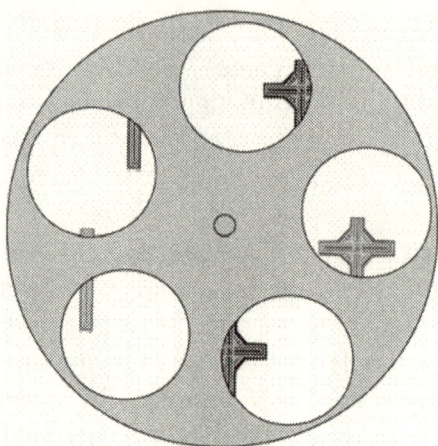

Figure Four – Progressive Revelation model

In Progressive Revelation, students see a few bits and pieces here and there in the Old Testament that may be useful for our Christian faith. The reason they see so little is because the model they are using won't let them see the whole picture in each window. And if we already think that it's supposed to be fragmentary by nature, who will be looking for a complete picture?

And it's particularly misleading to try to fit the bits and pieces from different windows into a whole picture, as if the bit in one window must fit together with the piece in another window. The Historical Redemptive approach attempts to see a progression between parts of stories instead of seeing them in their context as a complete doctrinal lesson.

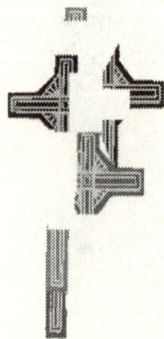

Figure Five – Progressive Revelation's picture of Christ

But if you turn the top wheel a bit more clockwise, the full pictures on the disk underneath appear as they really are.

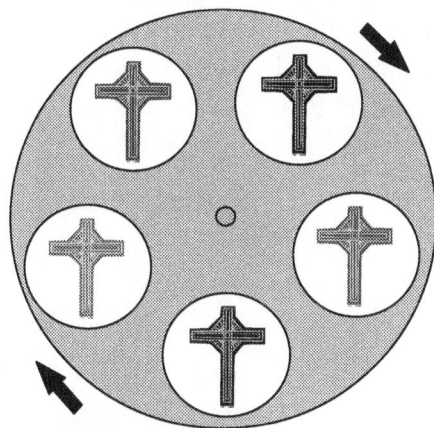

Figure Six – Distributed Revelation model

Now it's easy to see that each window shows a complete picture in itself. The window is deliberately designed to uncover the picture in all its details – each colored cross shows something about Christ from a new point of view. If we know this is the design of the Old Testament, then we'll be looking for this.

In the same way, the Progressive Revelation model would lead one to believe that in each of the stories of the Old Testament we have only a few fragmentary details about the knowledge of God – certainly not enough in any story to create a full doctrinal lesson about Christ. But if we look at the Old Testament through the Distributive model, each story becomes a complete description of a particular aspect of the person and work of Christ – so much so that we can't afford to put it aside, even when crossing over into the New Testament.

On an assembly line, functioning, working components are put together to make a car. The car doesn't consist of only the motor or wheel well; but neither is the motor deficient, or the wheel well poorly designed for the need at hand. Each part is perfect in itself; and when assembled into the complete car, the parts work together to make the car do what we want.

In the same way, each Old Testament story and section serves a vital function in describing the complete work of Christ. None of the parts of the Old Testament are sufficient in themselves to fully describe Christ (which Progressive Revelation correctly teaches, but as a result of its "organic" emphasis it led people to doubt the adequacy of each part to describe the person and work of Christ). But we can't have a true understanding of Christ without each part. We can illustrate it like this:

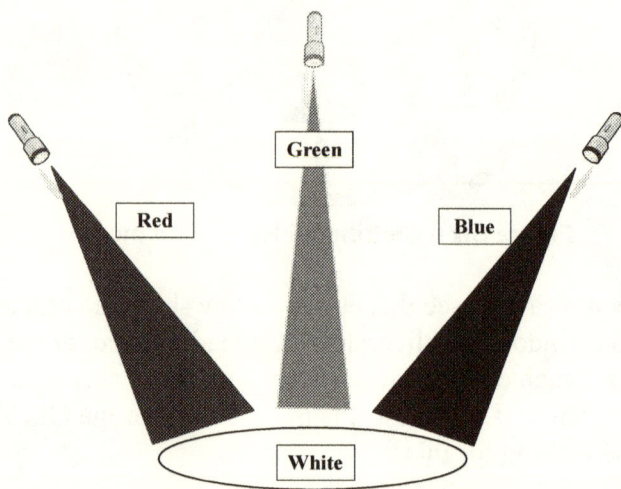

Figure Seven – Three colors make white

Three colors together make white light. Obviously red light exists; but the red light by itself doesn't give us the whole scope of the electromagnetic spectrum, nor is it immediately obvious that it would blend with other colors to make white light. But it does give us important information about the part of the spectrum that it covers – other colors lack that "red" data. The Old Testament stories, unfortunately, are too often divorced from the message of the whole Bible, as if they were Jewish incidents and therefore have little to do with the Christian faith. Each story is an important lesson in itself, and must be studied for its own message. But it was never meant to stand alone. The overall theme of the Bible is Christ, and each story provides an essential doctrinal piece to that theme that other parts don't give us.

It's true that the Old Testament stories were "shadows" of the reality in Christ.

> They serve at a sanctuary that is a copy and shadow of what is in Heaven. This is why Moses was warned when he was about to build the tabernacle: "See to it that you make everything according to the pattern shown you on the mountain." (Hebrews 8:5)

But that doesn't therefore mean that the shadow didn't give us enough information about Christ, that the "full realization" of the *doctrine* of Christ can only be understood in the New Testament. ***The important details that we need to know about that particular aspect of Christ are found in each Old Testament story.*** The idea of a shadow doesn't take away from its teaching efficacy; rather it points out the lack of substance, in this case the power behind the system. Though they knew the data about salvation in Christ, it requires the Person to make it efficacious.

What we get in the New Testament is the realization that all these doctrinal concepts have a Name; they describe a unique being who encompasses the entirety in himself. We see the *glory* of these truths in the Son of God, and we now have someone in whom to *hope*. The Old Testament described a huge system that was beyond the efforts of man to manage, though all of it was essential. The New Testament gave us someone who can manage it for us successfully.

It is crucial to realize that the Old Testament lays the groundwork for truly understanding the New Testament. Unless we get our Christian doctrine from the Old, and use these to guide our understanding of the New, our "faith" will be simply wrong. For example, many in the Church think that conversion is just a matter of "believing in Jesus." Evangelistic services center mainly around this duty on the sinner's part. The texts used to encourage people to do this are "Believe in the Lord Jesus, and you will be saved – you and your household," and others like it.

But in Genesis 1 we are told how God first created the world – through three primary methods: his Word, by miracle, and by command. It's significant that the New Testament picks up the theme of Creation and uses it to define our conversion as Christians – Paul calls us the "new Creation," Jesus is the "second Adam" who is the beginning of a new race, and the heavens and earth will be made new. If we are not to miss the point entirely, we *must* apply the same process of the first Creation to the second Creation. A person becomes a Christian, he is born again, he is made new, he is converted – by means of God's Word, by miracle at the hand of God, and by God's command. The current evangelistic emphasis is on the work and will of man; the Bible's is on God's work and will. A revival depending on the former will show poor results in the long run; but a revival using methods based on the latter will be more permanent and effective.

Therefore, without the Old Testament lessons we are going to misinterpret and misuse New Testament practices. [8] The Bible does say, for example in Acts 15:11, that salvation is of the Lord. But while we willingly acknowledge that fact, we really don't have any good understanding of why it's true without the Old Testament explanation.

Keep in mind that, at all times throughout the Old Testament, this was God speaking to the Israelites. The authority of the source gives authority to the book. What God said was binding on them:

> We must pay more careful attention, therefore, to what we have heard, so that we do not drift away. For if the message spoken by angels was ***binding***, and every violation and disobedience received its just punishment, how shall we escape if we ignore such a great salvation? (Hebrews 2:1-3)

And, if it was binding, then nothing essential to their salvation was missing. Otherwise God would be unjust to condemn them.

---

[8] This example amply demonstrates the fact that we are *not* reading our Christian doctrine back into Old Testament stories and then claiming that the Old Testament describes Christ! The Old truly does spell out many Christian doctrines for us, more clearly and systematically than we will get them in the New. Our wrong practices arise when we ignore the Old Testament foundation.

The role of the New Testament

The Old Testament does such a good job at laying out the truths of the Kingdom of God that there is really very little left for the New Testament to cover. Like David who drew up the blueprints for the Temple, collected materials, and then instructed Solomon to carry out his orders, Jesus came simply to carry out his Father's will – which was plainly set out for him already in the Hebrew Scriptures.

We first learned about sacrifice for sins in the Old Testament. We learned about true faith in the story of Abraham. The Law taught us what God expects of those who want to live with him; it's the perfect description of righteousness. Resurrection from the dead can be found in several places in the Old Testament. The saints of that time knew (at least those who had faith!) that the Kingdom that God is really interested in is a spiritual Kingdom, not a physical one. The Temple in Heaven was fully described by the Temple on earth. In the Old we learned about the Redeemer, and the Deliverer, and the High Priest. In the Old Testament we learn about the two kinds of work that the Holy Spirit does.

Even the name "Jesus" is first found in the Old Testament. "Joshua" is the Hebrew equivalent of the Greek name "Jesus." Of course there were several people who had the name Joshua in Old Testament times simply because it was a popular name (just as many Hispanics bear the name "Jesus" in our day). But the Joshua who led the Israelites into the Promised Land didn't bear his name by accident; it was a preview of things to come in the spiritual Kingdom of God. Both names, in fact, come from an ancient Name of God that best described the God of Israel – "Jesus" is a combination of the words "Yahweh is salvation." It is first defined for us in Exodus 34:6-7, the first and best description in the Bible of how the God of love and holiness deals with sinners.

What is even more fascinating is that the Old Testament describes the special work that Jesus would do as Priest and King – one man carrying both responsibilities. This is an idea that seemingly would have been strictly a New Testament theme, due to its sensitive nature to the Jew.

Take the silver and gold and make a crown, and set it on the head of the high priest, Joshua son of Jehozadak. Tell him this is what the LORD Almighty says: "Here is the man whose name is the Branch, and he will branch out from his place and build the temple of the LORD. It is he who will build the temple of the LORD, and he will be clothed with majesty and will sit and rule on his throne. And he will be a priest on his throne. *And there will be harmony between the two*." (Zechariah 6:11-13)

So we are taught that in Jesus both functions will come together – priest and king. In former days, the king of Israel came from the tribe of Judah, and the priest from the tribe of Levi. But if Jesus takes on the responsibility for both jobs, that would have raised some eyebrows among the legalists who want to see the organization run according to the Book (see an example of this in 2 Chronicles 26:16-21). But by God's decree here in Zechariah *one* man *will* be both Priest and King, and his Name will be called – Jesus!

There are actually only two *new* concepts that the New Testament deals with, things that the Old Testament saints had never dreamed of. In fact these two things caught the Jews completely off guard; they stumbled over these two points. In themselves they are staggering concepts, so it's no wonder that the entire New Testament is devoted to them. They are the finishing touch to God's system of salvation that was so laboriously developed in the Old Testament. The Apostles (by means of the Spirit of God) grasped the importance of these two points and how necessary they are to finish and even make possible the solution to sin and death. Without them the great Jewish system would have ground to a halt; with them, it becomes Christianity.

The point of the New Testament can be put like this:

**The New Testament reveals the New Man,
and how we become one with him.**

44

God's sole aim throughout history was the restoration of man. What he wants is for us to be perfect again, as he originally designed us. And in the Old Testament he worked out a plan that will erase our past, purify our hearts, and make us fit to live with him forever. What was lacking, however, was the motive power that would make it work. The Jews, even knowing all the details about salvation, never succeeded in following all the necessary steps. Everyone failed God somewhere along the line, in some way.

So God did it himself. The *first new concept* that the New Testament has for us is that God became a man. The incarnation of Christ was something that the Old Testament never described in doctrinal form as it does the rest of our faith. That's why the Jews reacted so violently against Jesus' statements about having come from his Father in Heaven. But it was a vital step in the plan, because without it we could never be saved from sin and death. We knew that God planned to solve our problem by himself from several key OT passages (for example, see Isaiah 63:6), but becoming a man was a surprise.

This is in fact a testing point – a Shibboleth, if you will – of our faith.

> This is how you can recognize the Spirit of God: *Every spirit that acknowledges that Jesus Christ has come in the flesh is from God*, but every spirit that does not acknowledge Jesus is not from God. This is the spirit of the antichrist, which you have heard is coming and even now is already in the world. (1 John 4:2-3)

This New Man enters the Bible in the Gospels full of the power of the Spirit – which was the motive force that was necessary to make the Old Testament system work. Jesus obeyed the Law to the letter, to its very depths; this is something that God has wanted to see a man do since the beginning of time. Jesus loved his Father and lived solely to do his will. He loved men and worked day and night for their physical and spiritual benefit. He hated sin. He fought the enemy with the power of the Spirit and won all confrontations. He was filled with wisdom and insight. His entire life was holy – that is, set apart for God's use alone.

Nobody else could have done this as the Son of God did. For thousands of years the Jews tried and failed to please God living under the Law. But Jesus was different; in a single lifetime he achieved what generations of Israelites couldn't do before him. "This is my Son, whom I love; with him I am well pleased." (Matthew 3:17)

Now that a perfect life had been lived according to the high standards of God's Law, Jesus could pay the price for our sins. His death – the death of a righteous man – was the sacrifice that finally appeased the wrath of God against sinners. A substitute (which the Law allows, because of the mercy of God) took our punishment upon himself so that we might be set free from condemnation. Again, this is not a concept that could be developed in the Old Testament. No man's life was precious enough to God to substitute for ours; only the life of the Son of God would move God's heart.

To finish the job, God raised Jesus from the dead into eternal life, and lifted him high above all things in the universe – to his own right hand, sitting on the throne of Heaven. Now a *man* sits as co-regent with God! The resurrection of Christ wasn't just for his own sake, but was a key step in *our* salvation. It's not as if Jesus wanted to do any of this for his own benefit; he already had a perfect life with the Father before the world was made. He became a man so that *we* might become one with God. He did this so that we might be saved.

That's the **second concept that is new** in the New Testament. The Old Testament continually preached the need for us to be holy, to be righteous, to live for the will of God – but it never imagined that God would do something staggering to make it possible and bring us to Heaven to be his children. To make sure we become holy and stay that way forever, God's solution is to make us *one with Christ* the Holy One, his Son. We have become part of his very body, his life. Now we can't fail! Now wherever Jesus goes, we go with him; whatever he does, we do with him. He became heir of God's Kingdom and so do we who are united with him. He became the second Adam, the firstborn of a new race destined for the Throne of Heaven.

46

If this is our destiny, how in the world are we going to become one with Christ? It's not going to be an Eastern religion experience where spirits just meld together and become one big spiritual nebula. The answer lies in the work of the Holy Spirit. He was always there in the Old Testament, just below the surface of everything that God did with his people. What nobody knew was how integral the Holy Spirit would be to our salvation. There is nothing in the Old Testament that teaches us that the Spirit of Christ is going to enter our spirits and make us one with Christ: this is strictly a New Testament theme. Jesus lives in us through his Spirit, and we live in him.

This is the mystery that the Apostles revealed to the Church.

> I have been crucified with Christ and *I no longer live, but Christ lives in me*. The life I live in the body, I live by faith in the Son of God, who loved me and gave himself for me. (Galatians 2:20)

> I have become its servant by the commission God gave me to present to you the word of God in its fullness – the *mystery* that has been kept hidden for ages and generations, but is now disclosed to the saints. To them God has chosen to make known among the Gentiles the glorious riches of this mystery, which is *Christ in you*, the hope of glory. (Colossians 1:25-27)

Jesus longed for the day when he could bring his "sheep" together and they would have fellowship with himself and with the Father – by becoming one with him.

> I pray also for those who will believe in me through their message, that all of them may be one, Father, just as you are in me and I am in you. May they also be in us so that the world may believe that you have sent me. I have given them the glory that you gave me, that they may be one as we are one: I in them and you in me. May they be brought to complete unity to let the world

47

know that you sent me and have loved them even as you have loved me. (John 17:20-23)

The act of making us one with Christ is a mystery indeed; nobody can understand how it works or how to make it happen. (See John 3:8 on this.) But the Creator who made the world knows how to recreate us in his image – a second Creation, not able to fall into sin and death again but able to live in the presence of God forever. Making the Son of God a man was the open door for humanity to live with God. The way that you and I can take advantage of this new opportunity is to become one with Christ, the righteous Man, through the Spirit.

If you think that these are difficult concepts to grasp, you're right. Even the angels long to look into these things! And since God knew we would need help understanding the mystery of the Gospel, he gave us Apostles to explain it to us. You will also notice that they don't spend much time on the basics – they're too busy explaining the new material, which is difficult enough to understand. They assume that the reader has done his homework already in the Old Testament.

> We have much to say about this, but it is hard to explain because you are slow to learn. In fact, though by this time you ought to be teachers, you need someone to teach you the elementary truths of God's word all over again. You need milk, not solid food! Anyone who lives on milk, being still an infant, is not acquainted with the teaching about righteousness. But solid food is for the mature, who by constant use have trained themselves to distinguish good from evil.

> Therefore let us leave the elementary teachings about Christ and go on to maturity, not laying again the foundation of repentance from acts that lead to death, and of faith in God, instruction about baptisms, the laying on of hands, the resurrection of the dead, and eternal judgment. And God permitting, we will do so. (Hebrews 5:11 – 6:3)

The disciples of Jesus (who were later the Apostles – the "ones sent out") were hand-picked eyewitnesses who spent three years with

Jesus. They saw his works, they listened to his lessons, they pondered over the events surrounding the life of Christ. But even they had little idea of what was happening ... until the Spirit of God filled them at Pentecost. Then the mystery was made plain to them and they had supernatural ability to carry the *right* message to the nations. They saw the truth about **the nature of Christ** and they knew the steps that one should take **to become one with the Son of God**. The data was the same as before; but now they became the teachers of the Church. We understand the true nature of Christ and his work through their teachings.

> Consequently, you are no longer foreigners and aliens, but fellow citizens with God's people and members of God's household, **built on the foundation of the apostles and prophets**, with Christ Jesus himself as the chief cornerstone. (Ephesians 2:19-20)

Since the Spirit of Christ is the key to being one with Christ, the Apostles explain difficult but critical concepts like being filled with the Spirit, walking in the Spirit, not grieving the Spirit, and bearing spiritual fruit.

They also teach us a great deal about the New Creation. They don't want us to make the same mistake that the Jews made, thinking that the old physical system is God's ultimate goal for his people. The Epistles of the New Testament contrast the old world with the new world; they show us Heaven, and the glory of God in the Church. They press upon us the need for conversion of the soul, not just outward conformity to the Law. Of course all this was taught in the Old Testament, but now the time had come to cut the cord with the physical and implement the spiritual Kingdom.

And speaking of the Jews, one point that the Apostles were careful to make clear is that anybody can come to Christ for salvation and the New Creation – not just the Jews. The promise was always there in the Old Testament that God would eventually extend his plan around the world; the Jews were the first to learn about his Kingdom, but they are not the *only* ones allowed into God's Kingdom! It was always predicted that the Gentiles would eventually come into the family of God; but the Old Testament never fully explained how that was to happen. The reason for that is that it requires an understanding of the second mystery that the Apostles revealed to the world: that to become spiritual children of God, we must become one with Christ. In other words, it's not enough to be a Jew, but you must become a Christian – and both Jew and Gentile must do that to be an heir of Abraham.

> His purpose was to create in himself one new man out of the two, thus making peace … He came and preached peace to you who were far away and peace to those who were near. For through him we both have access to the Father by one Spirit. Consequently, you are no longer foreigners and aliens, but fellow citizens with God's people and members of God's household. (Ephesians 2:15, 17-19)

The Apostles were actually interpreters of Christ. Like the Pharisees, it was entirely possible to look at Jesus of Nazareth and miss the point about him. Because he came as a man, it was easy to miss his true glory. Only by faith can we see the Son of God in Jesus and his work. But just in case we missed the point in the Gospels from Jesus' teaching, the Apostles also focus on that point in their letters. There should be no mistaking their message: the Messiah has come to gather his people to himself and take them to Heaven. The old promises that God made to his people are true; but the *way* he plans to fulfill them is completely unexpected – this time it's going to work.

Physical versus spiritual

One of the most important aspects of the Bible is how the physical and spiritual levels interact with each other in the timeline of God's works.

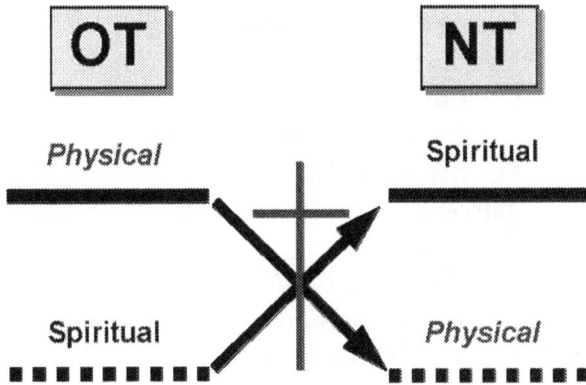

Figure 8 – Physical versus Spiritual

• In the **Old Testament**, the *physical* level predominates. We see animal sacrifices in a physical Temple. We see the children of Israel settling down in Canaan. We watch David pulling the tribes together and defeating the Moabites and Philistines. Just about everything we read about is something that we can see, feel, or hear with our physical senses.

God did this for a reason. Since the solution to mankind's problems of sin and death is so complex – and since the ultimate solution is a spiritual one which nobody can see – he started out by teaching us the answer on a level that we could easily grasp. It's amazing how much children can learn if you make your point in the form of stories and pictures.

So to teach us lessons of his spiritual world in terms of which we cannot mistake the meaning, he used stories describing his works in the lives of real people in real places. The point is there for anybody to see; a child can understand the story; and if we read and believe what God is saying, we can be saved.

Some of the important stories of the Bible include the following:

The Creation of the world
Abel's sacrifice
The Flood
The Covenant with Abraham
The Blessing of Jacob
Deliverance through Joseph
The Exodus
The Promised Land
David and Solomon
The Divided Kingdom
Punishment and Exile
Rebuilding the Temple and the walls of Jerusalem

We miss the point, however, if we think that these events (and many others) were merely physical events that happened for the benefit of the Old Testament saints only. The Bible was written for all of us; the whole Church is the recipient of God's letter. The physical events recorded in the Old Testament describe the same things that happen in God's spiritual world *in all ages*.

Though the physical level predominates in the Old Testament, we can catch a glimpse of the spiritual just behind the physical, right underneath the surface, if we have the eyes to see and ears to hear. Passages like the following show us that God always did consider the physical level to be temporary and not the ultimate point:

> "The multitude of your sacrifices – what
> are they to me?" says the LORD. "I have more
> than enough of burnt offerings, of rams and
> the fat of fattened animals; I have no pleasure
> in the blood of bulls and lambs and goats."
> (Isaiah 1:11)

Didn't he tell the Israelites to bring these sacrifices to him at the Temple? Yet here he is claiming that he hates them! The point is that they were hiding behind the animal sacrifice as if that would buy them a reprieve from the condemnation of the Law, and then going right back into their sin. This is not the way to worship God! The sacrifices were designed to teach us how terrible is the effect of sin. We're supposed to stop our sinning. If anything, the sacrifice would point up the need for something more permanent that would change the heart, so that we wouldn't sin anymore. The sacrifices of the Temple were an embarrassing reminder of the weakness of the system. (See Romans 8:3 and Hebrews 10:1-4 on this point.)

Paul also gives us clues revealing that some of the Old Testament saints understood the ultimate goal of a spiritual kingdom.

> A man is not a Jew if he is only one outwardly, nor is circumcision merely outward and physical. No, a man is a Jew if he is one *inwardly*; and circumcision is circumcision of the *heart*, by the Spirit, not by the written code. Such a man's praise is not from men, but from God. (Romans 2:28-29)

> The LORD your God will *circumcise your hearts and the hearts of your descendants*, so that you may love him with all your heart and with all your soul, and live. (Deuteronomy 30:6)

It was always understood, by those who had the faith of Abraham, that the physical symbols were lessons pointing to the spiritual realities in God's Kingdom.

• In the **New Testament**, the *spiritual* level predominates. The situation flip-flops, so to speak. Now instead of a physical Temple, we learn of the Temple in Heaven that we must come to. Now instead of a physical land of Canaan to inherit, we inherit Heaven. David sitting on his throne in Jerusalem turns into the Son of David sitting on his throne beside the Father. The Philistines aren't a problem to us anymore, but our sins and the "spiritual forces of darkness" certainly are.

Of course the situation in the Old Testament was also spiritual, but they were required to learn and work things out through the physical means that God gave them. Only by faith would they realize that a more permanent solution from Heaven would eventually come to light on earth. Now, however, the veil has been taken away, the time has come; the eternal solution has been revealed to us.

> These were all commended for their faith, yet none of them received what had been promised. God had planned something better for us so that *only together with us would they be made perfect*. (Hebrews 11:39-40)

The Gentiles need to learn the lessons of the Old Testament so that they can understand their faith. The Jews need to graduate from their physical system so that they can finally enjoy the spiritual reality of God's salvation. Either way, we don't need the physical anymore. It has served its purpose; the lessons are now recorded in the Old Testament for all to learn. Those lessons are a stepping stone, a primer to something better. Why long for the shadow when you can have the real thing? That's why the Apostles urged us to leave the physical behind and, through faith, reach out for the eternal realities:

> The blood of goats and bulls and the ashes of a heifer sprinkled on those who are ceremonially unclean sanctify them so that they are outwardly clean. How much more, then, will the blood of Christ, who through the eternal Spirit offered himself unblemished to God, cleanse our consciences from acts that lead to

death, so that we may serve the living God! (Hebrews 9:13-14)

We do have a few minor physical aspects to our religion, however. We gather together in church buildings, we are baptized with water, we eat bread and drink wine at the communion service, we have preachers and teachers who train us with the Word of God. But we understand (or we're supposed to!) that these can't touch the soul like the Holy Spirit can. The reality isn't in the things we use in our religion; those are "vessels" through which God touches us with the treasures from Heaven. We know now that we can pray anywhere, not just in Jerusalem – because the Spirit lifts us up to the Throne of Heaven.

> Believe me, woman, a time is coming when you will worship the Father neither on this mountain nor in Jerusalem. You Samaritans worship what you do not know; we worship what we do know, for salvation is from the Jews. Yet a time is coming and has now come when the true worshipers will worship the Father in spirit and truth, for they are the kind of worshipers the Father seeks. God is spirit, and his worshipers must worship in spirit and in truth. (John 4:21-24)

The list of physical concepts that God used to lead Israel is still important to us, but now on a spiritual level.

Physical	Spiritual
The Creation of the world	*The New Creation*
Abel's sacrifice	*The sacrifice of Christ*
The Flood	*This world will be destroyed*
The Covenant with Abraham	*The Gospel of Christ*
The Blessing of Jacob	*Treasures in Heaven*
Deliverance through Joseph	*Deliverance through Christ*
The Exodus	*Leaving the world behind*
The Promised Land	*Heaven*

David and Solomon	King Jesus
The Divided Kingdom	Division in the Church
Punishment and Exile	Discipline of God's people
Rebuilding the Temple and the walls of Jerusalem	Rebuilding the Church

Remember that this is a short list; there are so many lessons to be learned in the Old Testament and they all have spiritual counterparts in Christ's Kingdom. God's Kingdom used to be on earth, among the Jews, and they first learned what it's like to live with this God. Now the Church is living with him, and they too must learn the same lessons. We are all in training for living with a spiritual God that we can't see or touch.

The strength of the Distributed Revelation model

The benefits of a new model will be evident immediately in the way it opens up the field for new, exciting research. The old model leads us into dead ends and contradictions; the new model puts strength and authority into the work and message of the Church – we can understand our source of information better now, and can bring relevant truths to the circumstances of life.

- The new model for studying the Bible recognizes the authority of the entire Bible – not just select portions of the New Testament. When God spoke, either during the time of the Israelites or through Christ and his Apostles, he meant for us all to take notice and learn from him. One part of the Bible isn't more authoritative than another; he expects obedience from every age concerning all parts of the revelation of Christ dating from the times of Genesis to the times of the Apostles.

- The new model opens up the entire Bible for research and application. It particularly makes the Old Testament a virtual gold-mine of new ideas and resources for our Christian faith. If we recognize that the essentials of our Christian faith are distributed throughout the stories and events of the Bible, it will be both profitable and instructive to dig through the material with that in mind. It makes a great deal of difference what model you are using as you read the different sections of the Bible: if you think you're your faith is perfectly described only in the New Testament, you won't pay much attention to the Old Testament stories. However, if you know that your faith is best described, and many of its elements *only* described, in the Old Testament stories, you will be more alert to what is going on.

- The new model gives us a vital appreciation for the New Testament's reliance on the Old as a firm foundation for its message. The New Testament works on a complex and difficult aspect of our faith – the God-Man, and our spiritual union with him. It is part two of God's revelation to man. It can't make that point successfully, however, without relying completely on the full system of doctrine laid out in the Old Testament. Actually the Christian faith is not a separate religion from Biblical Judaism. We could call it a spiritualized form of the old Israelite faith, because it contains the very same principles as their religion, only raised to a spiritual level. The New Testament everywhere supports this premise.

Summary

We can summarize our findings in the following way:

A New Model for Biblical Studies

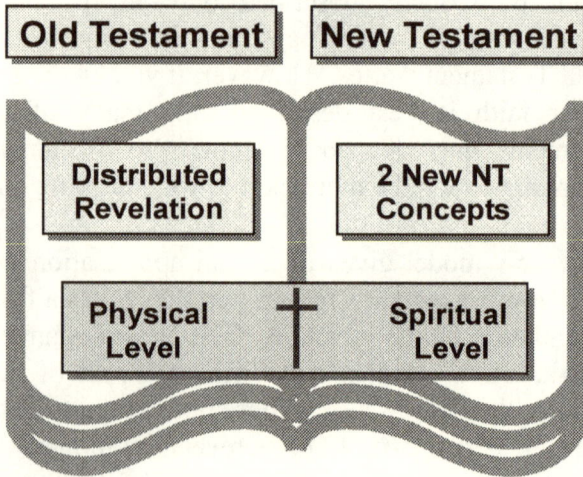

Progressive Revelation makes the Old Testament mostly irrelevant for the modern Christian, if not in theory then certainly in practice. The theory depends a great deal on how the Bible developed, because the message changed, grew and took form as history and culture progressed. The problem is that we can't take any of it too seriously until we get the "fully developed" form.

Distributed Revelation, however, cares little for how the Bible developed – it is, simply, the Word of God as it stands. Anything that isn't revealed to us in its pages is only man's conjecture anyway. In the Old Testament in particular, God gave us eternal truths by means of stories in historical context. These lessons fully reveal the person and work of Christ; our responsibility is to learn these lessons as they are and trust in him for what is written there. This is, in fact, the way Jesus and the Apostles regarded it. So, Distributed Revelation recognizes that the Old Testament is a vital source for Christian doctrine.

The New Testament relies on the groundwork laid in the Old Testament, but itself focuses on *two important concepts* that the Old

Testament could not cover – God come in the flesh, and our union with him through the Spirit. It also explains how we Gentiles are made part of a peculiarly Jewish system.

Finally, we must understand that the lessons in the Old Testament were deliberately put on a physical level so that we could understand a spiritual God and the way of access to his throne. Our hope, however, is not in this world – it never was. There will be a new heaven and a new earth, built on a spiritual foundation that will last forever uncorrupted.

Suggested books using the New Model

Mystery Revealed: A Beginner's Bible Survey

Eight Fundamentals of the Christian Faith

Ten Keys to the Bible

The Witness

Jesus and the New Testament

Removing the Veil: What the Old Testament Is All About

The Bible Explains Creation

Where the Paths Meet

Available from Ravenbrook Publishers – please visit the following website for more information

Ravenbrook Publishers

www.shenbible.org

www.ingramcontent.com/pod-product-compliance
Lightning Source LLC
Chambersburg PA
CBHW031333040426
42443CB00005B/324